Easy to Intermediate Piano Solo

THE WORLD'S GREAT CLASSICAL MUSIC

Classical Masterpieces

Transcribed for Easy Piano Solo / Intermediate Level

EDITED BY BLAKE NEELY AND RICHARD WALTERS

Cover Painting: Vermeer, *The Geographer*, 1668

ISBN 978-0-634-01267-9

HAL•LEONARD®
CORPORATION

7777 W. BLUEMOUND RD. P.O. BOX 13819 MILWAUKEE, WI 53213

Visit Hal Leonard Online at
www.halleonard.com

C O N T E N T S

4

ABOUT THE COMPOSERS...

JOHANN SEBASTIAN BACH (1685-1750).

Johann Sebastian Bach's incomparable genius for musical form and structure is revered more than 300 years after his birth. Yet the Baroque master and his music were actually forgotten by the general public and musicians alike for many years. Musical fashions were already changing by Bach's later years, and his music was heard less frequently than earlier in his lifetime. After his death, which may have been hastened by treatments and surgery for blindness, his music fell out of fashion. His second wife, Anna Magdelena, died in poverty about ten years later. Bach's works span a wide range of genres. He wrote liturgical works, Lutheran masses, church and secular cantatas, chamber music, organ works, orchestral pieces, concertos, vocal and choral pieces as well as compositions for clavier. In his day he was widely known as a virtuoso organist. His improvisational skills were legendary. With his contemporary George Frideric Handel, whom he never met, he was one of the last great composers of the Baroque era. Some ninety years after Bach's death, his works were once again brought before the public by the composer and conductor Felix Mendelssohn. Mendelssohn became a champion of the works of Bach and other composers who had been pushed aside with the shifting of musical fashions. Bach's music has been a mainstay of the international repertoire ever since.

LUDWIG VAN BEETHOVEN (1770-1827).

It is difficult to know how much of our perception of Beethoven is myth and how much is fact. He was the greatest composer of his era, certainly. Beethoven began his musical studies with his father, a Bonn court musician. He was appointed as deputy court organist in Bonn when he was eleven years old. He later continued his studies with Haydn, until differences between the two ended their relationship. Beethoven was first known to the public as a brilliant, flamboyant piano virtuoso, but there was a much darker aspect to his life. He was devastated when, in his late teens, he was summoned home from Vienna to keep vigil at his mother's deathbed. The second great tragedy of his life began when he was quite young, as a slight hearing impairment. Then in 1802, when the composer was 32, he was informed by doctors that he would eventually lose his hearing altogether. Beethoven sank into a deep despair, during which he wrote a will of sorts to his brothers. Whether or not he was considering suicide is a subject of some speculation. Whatever the case, the "Heiligenstadt Testament," as the will is known, states that he believed he would soon be dead. He eventually came to terms with his deafness and went on to write some of his most powerful pieces. His last six symphonies were written in the following years. In addition to his nine symphonies, Beethoven wrote pieces in nearly every imaginable genre. His works include an oratorio, two ballets, an opera, incidental music for various theatrical productions, military music, cantatas, a wealth of chamber music, 32 piano sonatas, various piano pieces, some 85 songs and 170 folksong arrangements. At Beethoven's funeral, on March 29, 1827, some 10,000 people joined in his funeral procession. One of the torch-bearers was composer Franz Schubert, who had idolized Beethoven. Some 45 years after his funeral, Beethoven's body was moved to Vienna's Central Cemetery, where he lies near the grave of Schubert.

HECTOR BERLIOZ (1803-1869).

Credited as the inventor of the modern orchestra, Hector Berlioz was one of the most original, creative composers of his age. He used phrases of irregular lengths, striking rhythms and inventive, colorful combinations of orchestral instruments to create new sounds using the traditional orchestral instrumentation. Although hailed today as the greatest French composer of the Romantic era, Berlioz was condemned during his lifetime as eccentric or simply wrong. Even as a young man, he managed to win the Prix de Rome on his fourth attempt—only by tempering his composition to follow a traditional style that would please the judges. As a child, Berlioz studied the flute and guitar. Following his father's wishes, he entered medical school, but after two years decided to follow his own career aspirations rather than his father's plans for his future. As a result, his father cut off financial support, leaving the young composer struggling for several years. Berlioz's career was a constant struggle for acceptance. In addition to composition he worked as a music critic and as a conductor. Berlioz was tremendously influenced by literary works, particularly by Shakespeare. Among his greatest orchestral works are *Symphonie fantastique*, *Harold en Italie* and *Roméo et Juliette*. Now hailed as the greatest of his five operas, *Les Troyens* (The Trojans) was not performed in French, in its complete version, until 1969. Although *Les Troyens* is not as long as the lengthier works of Wagner, and despite the fact that Berlioz intended it to be heard in a single performance, the opera is often split over two evenings when performed. Berlioz's eventual slide into depression and illness was exacerbated by the loss of his father, his two wives and his son as well as a number of friends. He became preoccupied with death, by some accounts longing to die. His music was not fully understood or appreciated until the twentieth century.

ALEXANDER BORODIN (1833-1887).

Alexander Borodin's success as a composer is astounding in the light of his double life. Borodin was a member of the "Moguchaya Kuchka" (Mighty Handful, or Mighty Five), a group of the five great Russian nationalist composers that included Balakirev, Borodin, Cui, Musorgsky and Rimsky-Korsakov. His works were known internationally during his lifetime and the "Polovetsian Dances," from his opera *Prince Igor*, remains a favorite in the classical repertoire today. The other side of Borodin's double life was an enormously successful career in medicine. As a child the composer taught himself the cello while pursuing a fascination with science. As an adult, his musical interests were always secondary to his research and lecturing. He taught at the Medico-Surgical Academy in St. Petersburg, traveling throughout Europe to give papers and lectures. Borodin allied himself with the Russian nationalists, making use of Russian folksongs and folk melodies in his works. He first achieved international recognition as a composer with *On the Steppes of Central Asia*. In addition to three symphonies, chamber music and vocal pieces, Borodin wrote five operas during his lifetime. Of the five, he completed only one, *Bogatïri* (The Bogatïrs). His greatest work was the opera *Prince Igor*, on which he worked from 1869 through 1887. Unfinished at the time of his death, the work was completed and partially orchestrated by Glazunov and Rimsky-Korsakov. Although it is based on Borodin's own libretto, which has been called weak and disjointed, the opera contains a great deal of remarkable music.

JOHANNES BRAHMS (1833-1897).

Johannes Brahms was a man of strong opinions. He disapproved of the "New German School" of composers, namely Liszt and Wagner. He avoided what he believed to be the excesses of the tone poem, relying instead on traditional symphonic forms. After his Symphony No. 1 was premiered, he was hailed as "Beethoven's true heir." The symphony, written when Brahms was forty-three years old, is so clearly linked to the symphonies of Beethoven that it has jokingly been called "Beethoven's Tenth." Brahms began his musical studies as a youngster, gaining experience in composition and working as an arranger for his father's light orchestra. He revered composer Robert Schumann. On the advice of Franz Liszt he met Schumann, with whom he developed a close friendship. He also developed a deep love for Schumann's wife, Clara Wieck Schumann. From the time of Schumann's mental breakdown until his death in 1856, Brahms and Clara tended to the ailing composer. The truth of the relationship between Brahms and Clara Schumann remains something of a mystery. Brahms never married. Clara Schumann never re-married following Robert's death. When Clara Schumann died in May of 1896, Brahms did not get to the funeral due to a missed train connection. He died the following April. Throughout his life, Brahms would sign letters "Frei aber froh" (Free but happy), until his last years when he signed "Frei aber einsam," (Free but lonely). One of the pall-bearers at Brahms' funeral was the composer Antonín Dvorák.

LÉO DELIBES (1836-1891).

The French composer and organist Léo Delibes made his living in various corners of the musical world before gaining recognition as a composer. He studied both organ and composition, taking his first job as a church organist at age 17. For a short time he worked as a music critic under the pen-name Eloi Delibès. Delibes' first stage work, the operetta *Deux Sous de Charbon*, premiered in 1856 when the composer was 19. Although he continued to work as an organist until 1871, Delibes focused his energies on the theater. From 1856, he wrote an operetta per year for about 14 years. He also worked as the chorus master at Théâtre-Lyrique for a time before becoming chorus master at the Paris Opéra in 1864. In 1866 his first ballet was performed. Although he had a reputation, during his lifetime, for witty, sophisticated operettas, he is best remembered today for his ballets. In 1881 Delibes took over from Max Reger as the professor of composition at the Conservatoire, despite his own admission that he knew nothing about theory and counterpoint. His ballet *Coppélia*, based on the work of E.T.A. Hoffmann, is among the most famous and loved pieces in the classical ballet repertoire. His opera *Lakmé* is considered his masterpiece. He died before finishing his grand opera *Kassaya*, which was later completed by Massenet.

ANTONÍN DVORÁK (1841-1904).

Antonín Dvorák's parents were firm believers that a child must learn to play an instrument and sing. Dvorák's father, an innkeeper by trade, was an avid amateur musician who played in the town band in Bohemia. But a career in music was unthinkable. The young Dvorák was expected to follow in his father's trade. After many battles the young musician was finally allowed to enter music school. After finishing his studies he took a job in an opera orchestra, taking on private students as well. By his mid-thirties he was supporting himself in great part with his compositions. Brahms, who later became his friend, helped him find a publisher for his work. His fame gradually spread throughout Europe and from there to the U.S. In 1885 Dvorák was invited to become director of the National Conservatory of Music in New York City. In his homeland, Dvorák had been both a fan and a student of folk music. In America he delightedly found a new style of folk music to study. He was particularly taken with the African-American spiritual. Yet he was homesick while in New York. Eventually he found a small Bohemian settlement in Spillville, Iowa, where he could spend his summers speaking his native tongue and generally relaxing in familiar cultural surroundings. In Spillville he worked on his Symphony No. 9, "From the New World." It was premiered in New York in 1893 and was a huge success. In 1895 homesickness took Dvorák back to Prague, where he became director of the Prague Conservatory. He continued to compose, but the disastrous premiere of his opera *Armida* in March of 1904 hurt him deeply. Two months later he died suddenly while eating dinner.

GABRIEL FAURÉ (1845-1924).

Like Beethoven, Gabriel Fauré suffered a gradual loss of hearing which he endeavored to keep a secret from both friends and colleagues. While many remained unaware of his deafness until after his death, his closest friends guessed the situation and ignored the composer's increasingly obvious condition. Fauré was widely respected during his lifetime as an organist and teacher. He was the director of the Paris Conservatory for many years, teaching composition to an entire generation of French composers. Among his pupils were Maurice Ravel and Nadia Boulanger, who would become the most influential composition teacher of the twentieth century. As one might suppose, Fauré had little time left over to devote to his compositional endeavors once his teaching and performing obligations were fulfilled. Summer holidays were his most productive times. He also had little time for romance, entering a marriage of convenience in his early forties. Fauré sought a distinctive voice in his compositions. Although he eventually found a delicate, restrained and understated style, it was slow to be appreciated by the public. He is now regarded as the greatest composer of French song.

CHARLES GOUNOD (1818-1893).

While French composer Charles Gounod was in Rome competing for the Prix de Rome, which he won on his third try in 1839, he discovered sixteenth-century polyphonic music wafting about the Sistine Chapel. He was so moved by this music, and likely by the setting as well, that he considered becoming a priest. Instead, he began composing masses and worked as a church organist in Paris. When he began writing operas, he leaned heavily on the examples of Gluck and Meyerbeer. Although these first operas were failures, he soon found his own voice, creating the likes of *Roméo et Juliette* and *Faust*. With *Faust* he struck a blow for French composers. *Faust*, although not a resounding success at the outset, was a powerful opera that came from the pen of a Frenchman. The opera put a dent in the domination of foreign operas in Paris and opened doors for other aspiring French composers. In the fifty years that followed, *Faust* was performed some two thousand times in Paris alone. It was the opera that opened the new Metropolitan Opera Company in New York in 1883. Gounod weathered the Franco-Prussian war living in England, becoming the first conductor of the Royal Albert Hall Choral Society. He returned to Paris in 1875, where he continued to work on operas. From 1881 to the end of his life he wrote almost exclusively church music. Like Mozart, he began a requiem that would prove to be his own. He was sitting at the piano, working on the Requiem, when he slumped onto the keyboard. He died three days later. Gounod's "Funeral March of a Marionette," written in 1873, is best known to television audiences as the Alfred Hitchcock theme.

EDVARD GRIEG (1843-1907).

Edvard Grieg holds a unique position in music history as not just the most famous of Norwegian composers, but as one of the only Norwegian composers to have achieved an international reputation. Grieg drew upon traditional Norwegian folksongs for the inspiration and basis for many of his pieces. His incorporation of national folk music into classical forms inspired musicians throughout Europe to do the same with the traditional music of their own countries. Although Grieg's Piano Concerto in A Minor is his best known work, it is not typical of his style. Most of his pieces are small in scale, giving him a reputation as a miniaturist. Grieg's first music lessons came from his mother. When Norwegian violinist Ole Bull heard the teen-aged Grieg play the piano, he arranged for him to enter the Leipzig Conservatory in Germany. Although the young musician was terribly homesick, living so far from home, he enjoyed the opportunity to hear performances by such luminaries as Clara Schumann and Richard Wagner. After his studies in Germany, and later in Denmark, Grieg returned to Norway. Finding himself in demand throughout Europe, Grieg spent much of his career traveling. The recipient of honorary degrees from Cambridge and Oxford, Grieg was also honored as one of his country's foremost composers.

GEORGE FRIDERIC HANDEL (1685-1759).

George Frideric Handel had the good sense to find a receptive audience for his music. Born Georg Händel, in Halle, Germany, the composer defied his father's wishes that he pursue law. He became known as a skilled keyboard player and respectable composer, and became a friend of the composer Georg Philipp Telemann. When his operas were not particularly well received in Hamburg, Händel moved to Italy. In 1711 he moved once again, this time to England. Two weeks after his arrival, the spectacle of his opera *Rinaldo* made him a famous man. The composer became a British citizen, changing the spelling of his name to suit his new nationality. The move to Britain proved fruitful, but life was not without its hardships. In 1715 he plunged from the height of success and popularity to absolute ruin. He not only survived, but rebuilt his reputation and once again achieved success. When it became apparent that he was played out as a composer of operas, he turned his attention to the oratorio, finding even greater success there than he had with his operas. He eventually lost his eyesight, which meant the end of his career as a composer. By then, his name firmly established, he turned his attention to conducting and performing as an organist. *Messiah*, certainly Handel's most famous work, composed in 1742, was both the last piece of music he would conduct and the last he would hear. He collapsed shortly after conducting a Good Friday performance of the seventeen-year-old oratorio. He died the following morning. According to his wishes, he was buried in Westminister Abbey. A statue at his grave depicts him in front of his desk, with quill pen in front of him. Lying on the desk is a score of *Messiah*, open to the soprano aria, "I Know That My Redeemer Liveth."

FRANZ JOSEPH HAYDN (1732-1809).

Born into the Baroque era, Franz Joseph Haydn came of age in the Classical era. He functioned as trailblazer, making the way for the likes of Beethoven, who was his student. He is remembered as the "father" of the modern symphony and the string quartet for his hand in establishing the forms of both. He was born to poor circumstances, yet his family saw his obvious talent and sent him to a nearby town to live in the home of a music teacher. Although life in his teacher's home was harsh, Haydn was well taught. He went on to sing in the boy's choir of St. Stephan's, where he remained until his voice broke at age seventeen. Once on his own, the young musician took a garret apartment and began working as a freelance musician, playing the violin and keyboard instruments and composing. He was eventually offered a court position, which he kept for a short time. When the Esterházy family, one of the most prominent Hungarian families, offered him a job as Vice-Kapellmeister, he immediately accepted. He remained in the employ of the Esterházy family for three decades, becoming full Kapellmeister in 1766. After the death of Nikolaus Esterházy, Haydn was granted a great deal of freedom to travel and to compose for persons other than the Esterházy family. Haydn wrote an astounding amount of music. He penned operas, chamber works, sacred music, over one hundred symphonies, as well as oratorios and even puppet operas. He was so prolific that even though his music is still frequently performed and his name is a household word in the world of classical music, the majority of his work remains unpublished and unknown.

GUSTAV MAHLER (1860-1911).

Gustav Mahler was not exactly a musician's musician. His perfectionism caused him to alienate many of the musicians with whom he worked. When he became music director of the Vienna Royal Opera he cleaned house, replacing orchestral singers and orchestral musicians. He restaged existing productions, seeing to every detail of the productions himself. The musicians considered him heavy-handed, while the opera's management felt he was spending money wildly. Mahler was a workaholic. He devoted his summers to composition since his conducting schedule during the concert season was non-stop. As a composer he devoted his energy entirely to songs, song cycles and symphonies. The symphonies are enormous, involved, Romantic works. They were brutally treated by the critics of his day. His symphonies did not find receptive audiences until after World War II, when they found unprecedented success. Mahler left the Vienna Royal Opera, sailing for New York to conduct at the Metropolitan Opera. While in New York he became instrumental in the revitalization of the New York Philharmonic. But his inability to slow down was taking its toll. Mahler had been warned that his heart was weak and was told to cut back on his working hours. Cutting back was impossible. He worked at his usual feverish pace until he collapsed in New York on February 21, 1911. Unable to return to work, he was moved to Paris for treatments. When it became apparent that he would not recover, he asked to be moved to Vienna where he died on May 18, 1911. The story has been told that in his last hours he conducted an imaginary orchestra with a single finger. It has also been said that his last word was "Mozart."

FELIX MENDELSSOHN (1809-1847).

While most of Mendelssohn's colleagues could tell stories of their battles with family over choice of career and even more tales of their financial struggles as musicians, Felix Mendelssohn could only listen. He was born into a wealthy family that supported his goals in music from the very first. Even in their conversion from Judaism to Christianity, which the family had long considered, they were spurred to action by thoughts of their son's future. It was at the time of their conversion that they changed the family surname to Mendelssohn-Bartholdy. Mendelssohn set out on his musical career with two clear goals. He wanted to re-introduce the largely forgotten music of old masters such as Bach to the public, and he dreamed of opening a first-rate conservatory. At the age of twenty he conducted a pioneering performance of Bach's *St. Matthew Passion*, the first of many such concerts he would lead. A few years later he founded and directed the Leipzig Conservatory. As a composer, Mendelssohn combined the expressive ideals of the Romantics with the traditional forms of the Classical era. He is remembered both as one of the great Romantic composers and one of the last of classicists. In his career Mendelssohn found success at an early age, and remained highly successful until his death. His sister Fanny, to whom he was exceptionally close, died suddenly on May 14, 1847. Shortly after he got the news of his sister's death, Mendelssohn fell unconscious, having burst a blood vessel in his head. Although he recovered from this incident, he was terribly diminished by the illness. His health and mental state deteriorated until his death on November 4 that same year. Memorial services for the great conductor/composer were held in most German cities, as well as in various cities in Great Britain, where he had become quite a celebrity.

10

WOLFGANG AMADEUS MOZART (1756-1791).

It is exceptional for nature to produce such a prodigy as Mozart. Playing capably at age three, composing at five and concertizing throughout Europe at age six, Mozart was clearly remarkable, even for a prodigy. But for nature to have placed two prodigies in one household is beyond belief. Mozart's sister Marianne (Nannerl), a few years older than Mozart, was also a prodigy and was also featured on these concert tours. The young musician's parents moved heaven and earth to further offer Mozart every opportunity to perform and study abroad. They traveled Europe incessantly. As an adult, Mozart had difficulties in his relationships with his employers, and with colleagues. Pop culture has presented us with a caricature image of the composer, thanks in great part to the film *Amadeus*, in which he is painted as a freakish, spoiled child who refused to grow up. He was, in fact, impetuous and, likely as a result of his star status as a child, often difficult to deal with. But there was more depth of personality and musicianship than the film attempted to convey. Mozart was known to complete an entire symphony in a single carriage ride, yet he chafed at accusations that it was not work for him to compose. Another factor in the exaggerated stories of his character was his inability to handle financial matters. Although he was well paid for many of his compositions, he was in constant financial difficulty. He was frequently forced to borrow money from family and friends. Mozart, who more than any other composer represents the Classical era, tried his hand at virtually every musical genre available, and succeeded across the board. In 1791 Mozart received a commission to compose a requiem. According to the terms, the source of the commission was to remain anonymous. The piece proved to be the composer's own requiem, in that he died of a 'fever" before it was completed. The circumstance of his death, and the anonymous commission, gave rise to great speculation at the time, and a film some two centuries later. In the mid twentieth century, the composer Richard Strauss is said to have laid a hand on a copy of Mozart's Clarinet Quintet and said, "I would give anything to have written this."

JACQUES OFFENBACH (1819-1880).

One of the finest tune-smiths of the nineteenth century, Jacques Offenbach helped define the genre of operetta. The international popularity of his operettas paved the way for the creations of such composers as Franz Lehár, Victor Herbert and the team of Gilbert and Sullivan. The operettas of Offenbach and others formed the roots of twentieth-century musical theater. Offenbach was raised in France, although his family was German in origin. Offenbach began his musical life with studies on the violin, switching to cello at a young age. Although his comic operas were a tremendous success both in France and abroad during the 1860s, the French civil war of 1870-71 triggered a change in musical taste. Following the war, Offenbach's operettas were no longer the rage they had once been. In 1876, in an effort to make some much needed money, Offenbach embarked on a tour of the United States. He played some forty concerts in the U.S., writing a book on his impressions of America upon his return to France. At the time of his death, Offenbach had completed 95 operettas and comic operas. He also wrote numerous vocal pieces and works for cello, as well as five ballets, additional dance music, vaudevilles and incidental music. Many of his operettas contain sharply witty lyrics that are punctuated by fairly blatant musical effects. Two of Offenbach's operas were unfinished at the time of his death: *Belle Lurette*, which was completed by Delibes, and his one serious opera, *Les Contes d'Hoffmann* (The Tales of Hoffmann), which was completed by Guiraud. *Les Contes d'Hoffmann*, considered his masterpiece, is still popular with opera companies throughout the world today.

HENRY PURCELL (1659-1695).

One of the greatest composers of the Baroque era and one of the greatest composers in English history, Henry Purcell found success in a wide range of musical formats. As the organist of Westminster Abbey and later the Chapel Royal, he composed and performed sacred music for services attended by British royalty as well as for public royal events. He turned his hand to theater music in about 1680. Since opera, as it was known in the rest of Europe, was not popular in England, he wrote incidental music for theatrical productions known as semi-operas. He wrote only one actual opera and one of the first written in the English language, *Dido and Aeneas*, for a girl's school in Chelsea. In addition to sacred music and music for royal events, Purcell wrote an enormous number of secular songs, many of which were published in songbooks during his lifetime. Although his works remained in publication and continued to be heard in performance (without the fall from public attention that the works of Bach and Vivaldi suffered), it was not until the 1878 formation of the Purcell Society that the composer's works were issued in a methodical, carefully catalogued fashion. Upon his death, Purcell was buried near the organ in Westminster Abbey, a clear indication of his position in British musical and religious circles. The last royal event for which Purcell composed music, was the funeral of Queen Mary in 1695. He died later that year.

SERGEI RACHMANINOFF (1873-1943).

Once described by composer Igor Stravinsky as "a six-and-a-half-foot-tall scowl," Sergei Rachmaninoff's stern visage was a trademark of sorts. Rachmaninoff first found fame as a pianist, touring throughout his native Russia to critical acclaim. His compositions won notice in those early years as well, including a Moscow Conservatory Gold Medal in composition. Yet the 1897 premiere of his Symphony No. 1 was a complete failure, due in large part to poor conducting by Alexander Glazunov. The dismal reception of the piece sent Rachmaninoff into a three-year creative slump that he overcame through hypnosis. During those three years he began conducting, earning international respect for his work on the podium. When his Symphony No. 1 received its London premiere in 1909, it was a huge success. Rachmaninoff made his first U.S. tour in 1909. On the tour he featured his Piano Concerto No. 3, which he had written expressly for his American audiences. Rachmaninoff fled Russia in the wake of the October Revolution of 1917. He brought his family to America where he continued to concertize, but did not compose for nearly a decade. After years of touring, Rachmaninoff decided that the 1942-43 concert season would have to be his last. In January of 1943 he began to suffer from an illness diagnosed as pleurisy. He gave what was to be his final performance on February 17. He then returned to his Beverly Hills home where he died of cancer on March 28.

NIKOLAY RIMSKY-KORSAKOV (1844-1908).

Trained as an officer in the Russian Navy, composer Rimsky-Korsakov had a great interest in music but little training beyond piano lessons. Although he displayed prodigious talents as a child, his aristocratic standing meant that a career in music was out of the question. Yet, after teaching himself counterpoint and harmony, and establishing himself as a composer, he became a professor at the St. Petersburg Conservatory. He was removed from that position when he publicly condemned the police control over the school and its students. Among his students were Alexander Glazunov and Igor Stravinsky. He is remembered as the central figure of "The Russian Five" (or "The Mighty Five"), a group of composers that included Modest Musorgsky, Alexander Borodin, César Cui and Mily Balakirev. The group favored a dynamic national style in distinct contrast to the elegant sounds of Tchaikovsky. Rimsky-Korsakov composed more than fifteen operas, numerous choral works and orchestral pieces, a great quantity of vocal music, as well as chamber works and piano pieces. Of this great quantity of music only three orchestral pieces have remained in the classical repertoire: the symphonic suite *Sheherazade* for which he is best remembered, his *Spanish Capriccio* and his *Russian Easter Festival*. Written in 1888, *Sheherazade* is based on vignettes from "Tales of the Arabian Nights."

GIOACHINO ROSSINI (1792-1868).

Acclaimed by his contemporaries as the greatest Italian composer of his time, Rossini enjoyed a measure of fame and wealth other composers could only envy. Having completed his first opera, *Demetrio e Polibio*, before the age of 16, Rossini wrote his last, *Guillaume Tell*, when only 37. Then, much to everyone's astonishment, he simply retired from opera composition. Rossini was born into a musical family; his mother was a singer and his father was a talented horn player. His abilities were apparent early on in his skillful singing and in a set of six delightful *Sonata a quattro* for strings, which he wrote around 1804. By the age of eighteen Gioachino had received his first opera commission. He worked feverishly to fulfill his many obligations, and in a period of just sixteen months composed seven operas, often borrowing tunes from one opera to plug into another. It was not uncommon for the same overture to serve for more than one opera. Sparkling melodies and buoyant rhythms, the hallmark of his style, are both in evidence in the famous William Tell Overture ("Lone Ranger Theme"). *Il barbiere di Siviglia* (The Barber of Seville), Rossini's masterpiece and perhaps the greatest of all comic operas, was composed in just three weeks and was an infamous failure on opening night. From 1829 until about 1857 the only compositions of significance were his *Stabat mater*, begun in 1832, and *Les soirées musicales* of 1830-35. In his last years, spent near Paris, Rossini wrote over 150 piano pieces, songs, and ensembles which he called *Péchés de vieillesse*, or "Sins of Old Age." His finest work from these years is the *Petite messe solennelle* for 12 voices, two pianos and harmonium, which he later orchestrated. Rossini died at his villa in November of 1868. His funeral was attended by thousands and memorials were held throughout France. In 1887 his body was moved to Florence.

CAMILLE SAINT-SAËNS (1835-1921).

Like Mozart, Camille Saint-Saëns was the sort of child prodigy that defies logical explanation. Able to read and write at age two, the young Saint-Saëns was composing as a three-year-old and performing recitals by age five. He made his formal debut at age ten, offering to play any of the thirty-two Beethoven piano sonatas from memory as an encore. Throughout his life, Saint-Saëns studied a wide variety of subjects. He was a respected writer in the fields of music, history and science. He was a virtuoso pianist, who played the organ with equal proficiency. Franz Liszt praised him as the world's greatest organist. Saint-Saëns was a prolific composer, writing operas, orchestral pieces, sacred and secular choral music, songs, chamber music and even a couple of pieces for band. In his younger years, the composer was an outspoken proponent of contemporary French compositions. He used his popularity and social standing to advance the careers of other composers, not his own. Yet in his middle and later years he not only ceased to support modern French composers, but became an outspoken opponent of the music of Debussy and later of Stravinsky. Along with Mendelssohn, he is credited with reviving neglected music of the past, bringing the likes of Bach, Handel, Gluck and Mozart before the public. Entitled "a grand zoological fantasy," *Carnival of the Animals* was neither published nor performed during Saint-Saëns' lifetime. This was by his own edict. In addition to characterizations of animals, he includes many musical quotations.

FRANZ SCHUBERT (1797-1828).

The story of Schubert's life reads like a heartbreaking novel. Now hailed as one of the great Romantic composers, not one of Schubert's symphonies was performed during his lifetime. It was five decades after his death before any of them were published. Schubert, the son of a school headmaster, was not a virtuoso musician. Although his musical abilities were readily apparent to his teachers, his inability to perform left him with little means to support himself. He taught in his father's school for a time, but was miserable in that job. Schubert studied with Salieri, who was astounded by the young composer's abilities. After writing his first symphony at age fifteen, Schubert presented Salieri with a completed, fully orchestrated opera two years later. Schubert lived less than thirty-two years, yet he composed a phenomenal amount of music, including some six hundred songs. One hundred and forty-four of those songs date from the year 1815, a year in which he was teaching at his father's school. After Schubert left his father's school, he had the good fortune to collect a small group of devoted friends and supporters. The friends would periodically organize evenings of the composer's music, which came to be known as "Schubertiades." Schubert's health began to fail as early as 1822. When he died, at age thirty-one, he was viewed as a composer of songs. It was not the enormous number of songs that earned him this mistaken designation so much as the fact that almost none of his other music had been performed during his lifetime. In addition to the songs, Schubert completed seven symphonies and left one unfinished. He wrote a number of operas, although these are far from his best works. He also wrote choral works, chamber music and piano pieces. In accordance with his dying wish, he was buried beside Beethoven, whom he had idolized and at whose funeral he had served as a torch-bearer.

ROBERT SCHUMANN (1810-1856).

Robert Schumann's dream was to become a pianist. As the son of a German bookseller and writer, he grew up surrounded by literature and instilled with a love of music. His world crumbled however, when he was just sixteen, with the death of his father and the subsequent suicide of his sister. Schumann entered law school, but spent most of his time studying music. In 1830 he moved into the household of his piano teacher, Friedrich Wieck. Soon afterwards, his left hand began to trouble him. His career dreams were shattered when his left hand became permanently crippled. He turned his energies to composition, making a name as a music critic as well. An inspired critic, he founded the music journal *Neue Zeitschrift für Musik*, in 1834; he often wrote under the pseudonyms "Florestan" and "Eusebius." Schumann fell in love with his teacher's daughter, Clara Wieck, a highly acclaimed concert pianist. Clara's father fought vigorously against the romance. Schumann married Clara in 1840, but only after he had taken his case to the courts. In the year he was married, the composer wrote some 150 songs, turning to orchestral music the following year. Schumann suffered from bouts of terrible depression, which became progressively worse with time. In 1854 he attempted suicide. Unable to function any longer, he was then placed in an asylum, where he spent the last two years of his life. His wife, along with his friend, the young composer Johannes Brahms, looked after him in those final years.

JOHANN STRAUSS, JR. (1825-1899).

Just as John Philip Sousa was America's March King, Johann Strauss Jr. was Austria's Waltz King. The Strauss family is synonymous with the waltz. Johann, Sr. was a violinist, conductor and composer, who was widely popular throughout Europe. He conducted in a flamboyant style, with violin in hand. He popularized the open-air concert and programmed many of his numerous works. His son Josef was also a conductor, working with the family orchestra and composing a number of pieces as well. Eduard, a younger son, became Vienna's imperial-royal music director from 1872-1901. He was the most respected conductor of the Strauss clan, and was in great demand throughout Europe. But it was Johann, Jr. who won the hearts of the Austrian people. His talent was recognized early and his first composition was published when he was only six years old. As an adult, he formed a rival orchestra to his father's and began to tour with his own music. Eventually the two groups were merged into a single family orchestra. While the public loved Johann, Jr., the world of classical music saw him as lacking substance. For all the criticism he received during his lifetime, his music is familiar to classical audiences a century after his death. During Johann, Jr.'s last days, the city of Vienna waited anxiously for hopeful news of his health. On June 3, 1899, a large crowd gathered for an outdoor concert. In mid performance, a messenger bolted onto the stage and whispered something into the conductor's ear. The conductor abruptly stopped the orchestra. After a few moments they began playing the opening notes of "By the Beautiful Blue Danube," Strauss' beloved waltz. The audience knew in an instant what it meant. Their Strauss had died. Rising to their feet, the men removed their hats and bowed their heads while women cried. A few days later, Johann Strauss, Jr.'s obituary referred to him as "the last symbol of cheerful, pleasant times."

PYOTR IL'YICH TCHAIKOVSKY (1840-1893).

It is a curious twist of fate that the composer of so bombastic a work as the *1812 Overture* should have been an extremely fragile individual. Exceptionally sensitive from childhood, Tchaikovsky eventually deteriorated into a precarious emotional state. Tchaikovsky's musical abilities were already quite evident by age five, as was his hypersensitivity. His mother died when he was fourteen, a painful event that some say prompted him to compose. Over the years he was plagued by sexual scandals and episodes we might call "nervous breakdowns" today. Historians have uncovered evidence that his death, which was officially listed as having been caused by cholera, was actually a suicide. Many believe that the composer knowingly drank water tainted with cholera. Tchaikovsky's work stands as some of the most essentially Russian music in the classical repertoire, yet he was not a part of the Russian nationalistic school. In fact he was treated quite cruelly by critics of his day. "Tchaikovsky's Piano Concerto No. 1, like the first pancake, is a flop," wrote a St. Petersburg critic in 1875. A Boston critic claimed that his Symphony No. 6 ("Pathétique") "...threads all the foul ditches and sewers of human despair; it is as unclean as music can well be." For all the vehement criticism the composer received during his lifetime, his works are now among the best loved of the classical repertoire. His ballet *The Nutcracker* is an international holiday classic, while *Swan Lake* is a staple in the repertoire of ballet companies throughout the world. His *1812 Overture* is among the most recognizable of all classical pieces. In 1893 the composer completed work on his Symphony No. 6. The first movement dealt with themes of passion, the second with romance, the third with disillusionment and the finale with death. The piece was premiered on October 28. Nine days later the composer was dead.

ANTONIO VIVALDI (1678-1741).

Antonio Vivaldi was very nearly forgotten by concert-going audiences until the early part of the twentieth century. It was violin virtuoso Fritz Kreisler who reminded the music world of Vivaldi's music by turning some of his themes into salon pieces. By the end of the twentieth century even those having no knowledge of classical music must have heard Vivaldi's *The Four Seasons* in the context of a motion picture soundtrack or a diamond commercial. Ordained as a priest in 1703, Vivaldi taught at a girls' school in Venice, writing for the orchestra and chorus of the school. He was known as the "red priest" owing to his vivid red hair. Vivaldi exerted a tremendous influence over German musicians, many of whom imitated his style. His creative concerto writing, complete with energetic repeated rhythmic patterns and unusual combinations of solo instruments, was one of his most important contributions. Yet history treated his remarkable output rather roughly. Russian composer Igor Stravinsky once noted that Vivaldi had written, "one concerto four hundred times." Considered the "father" of the modern concerto, Vivaldi's plan of three concerto movements (fast-slow-fast) set the standard for generations of composers to come. Vivaldi also wrote a great deal of vocal music, including more than forty operas. By the time of his death, his music had largely fallen out of fashion. He died a pauper, buried outside the Vienna city walls. One of a handful of singers at his funeral was the young Joseph Haydn.

Air on the G String

from the Orchestral Suite No. 3 in D

Johann Sebastian Bach
1685-1750
BWV 1068
originally for orchestra

Sheep may safely graze

from Cantata 208 ("Birthday Cantata")

Johann Sebastian Bach
1685-1750
BWV 208
originally for soprano,
2 flutes and continuo

Andante

Quia Respexit

from MAGNIFICAT

Johann Sebastian Bach
1685-1750
BWV 243
originally for soprano,
oboe d'amore and strings

Adagio

cresc.

mp

Wachet auf, ruft uns die Stimme

(Sleepers, wake)
from Cantata 140
Excerpt

Johann Sebastian Bach
1685-1750
BWV 140
originally for tenor,
strings and continuo

Moderate

[*mp*]

26

poco rit.

Symphony No. 3
"Eroica"
First Movement Excerpt

Ludwig van Beethoven
1770-1827
Op. 55
originally for orchestra

original key: E-flat Major

Symphony No. 7

First Movement Excerpt

Ludwig van Beethoven
1770-1827
Op. 92
originally for orchestra

original key: A Major

41

Symphony No. 9
Fourth Movement Excerpt

Ludwig van Beethoven
1770-1827
Op. 125
originally for chorus and orchestra

Allegro assai vivace

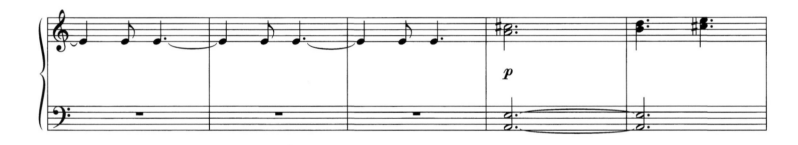

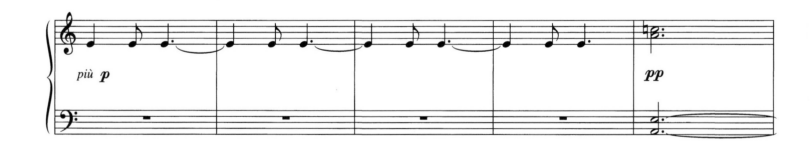

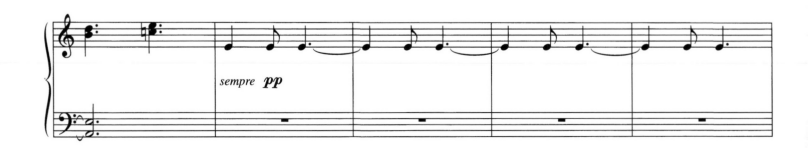

original key: D Major

44

Violin Concerto
First Movement Excerpt

Ludwig van Beethoven
1770-1827
Op. 61
originally for violin and orchestra

original key: D Major

March to the Scaffold

from SYMPHONIE FANTASTIQUE
Fourth Movement Excerpt

Hector Berlioz
1803-1869
Op. 14
originally for orchestra

Allegretto non troppo

Witches' Sabbath

from SYMPHONIE FANTASTIQUE
Fifth Movement Excerpt, "Dies irae" Theme

Hector Berlioz
1803-1869
Op. 14
originally for orchestra

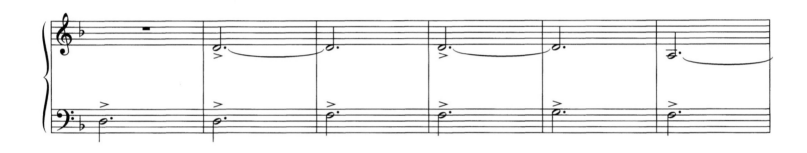

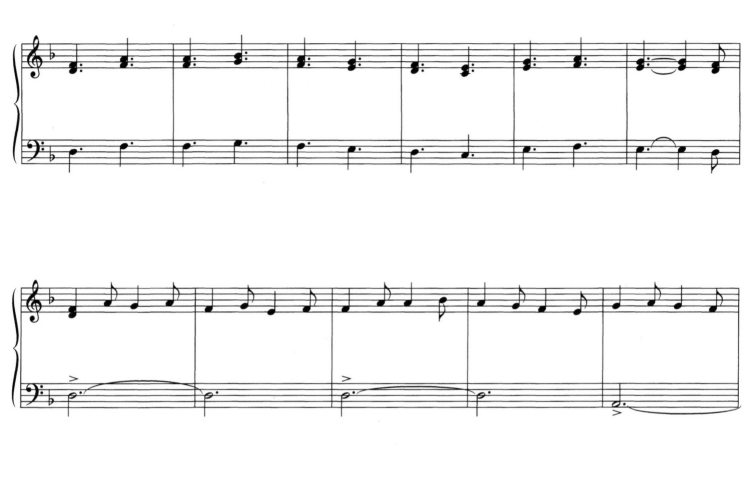

Polovetzian Dance

from the opera PRINCE IGOR
First Theme

Alexander Borodin
1833-1887
originally for orchestra

original key: A Major

Piano Concerto No. 2

First Movement Excerpt

Johannes Brahms
1830-1897
Op. 83
originally for piano and orchestra

Allegro non troppo

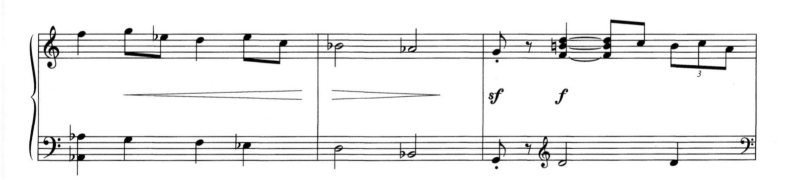

original key: B-flat Major

Symphony No. 3
Third Movement Excerpt

Johannes Brahms
1830-1897
Op. 90
originally for orchestra

Poco Allegretto

original key: C Minor

Pizzicato Polka
from the ballet SYLVIA

Léo Delibes
1836-1891
originally for orchestra

Pavane

Excerpt

Gabriel Fauré
1845-1924
Op. 50
originally for chorus and orchestra

original key: F-sharp Minor

Pie Jesu
from REQUIEM

Gabriel Fauré
1845-1924
Op. 48, No. 4
originally for soprano,
organ and orchestra

original key: B-flat Major

Slavonic Dance

Excerpt

Antonín Dvořák
1841-1904
Op. 46, No. 1
originally for piano, four hands
orchestrated by the composer

Ave Maria
"Meditation"
adapted from the Prelude in C by J.S. Bach

Charles Gounod
1818-1893
originally for chamber ensemble

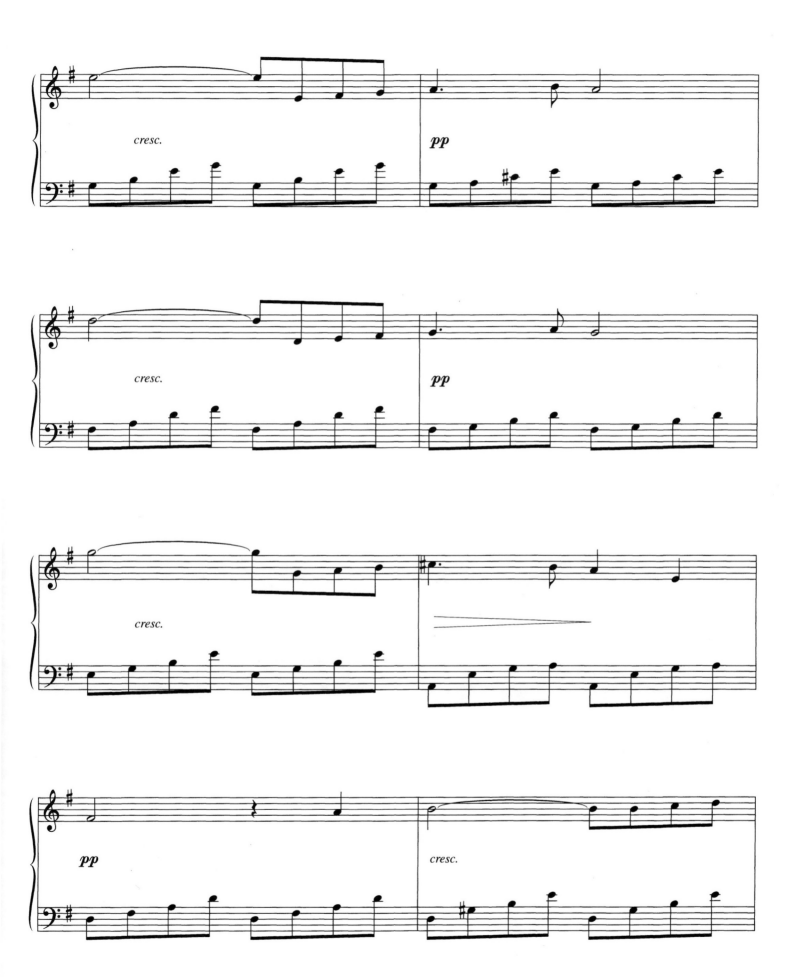

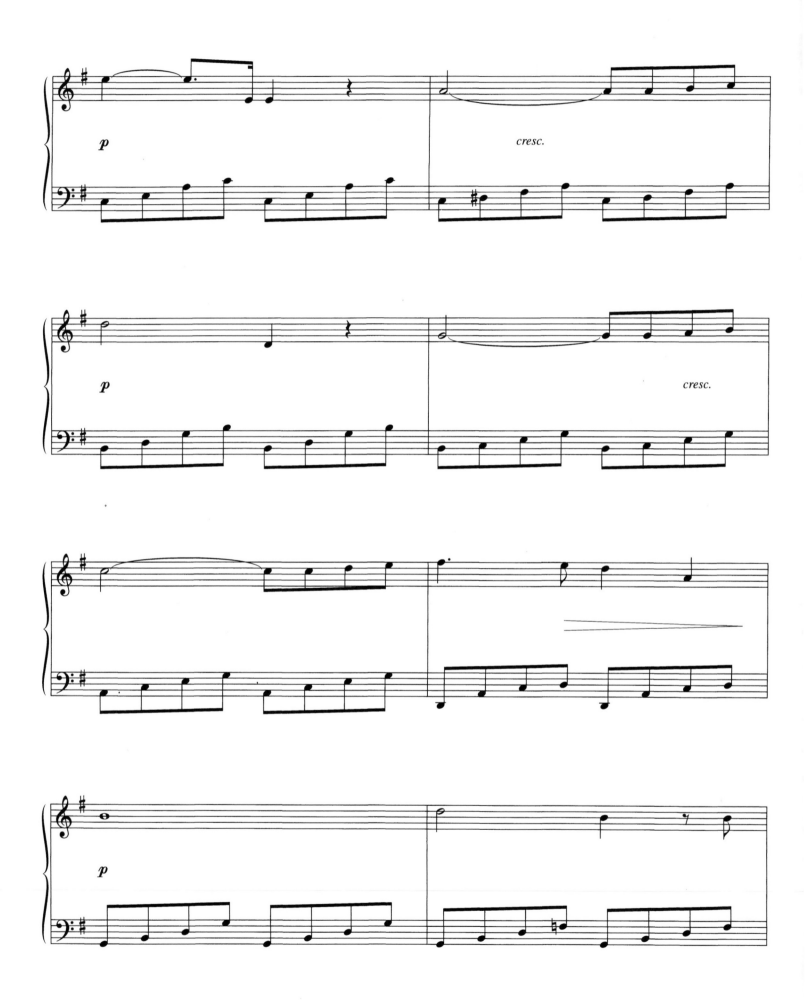

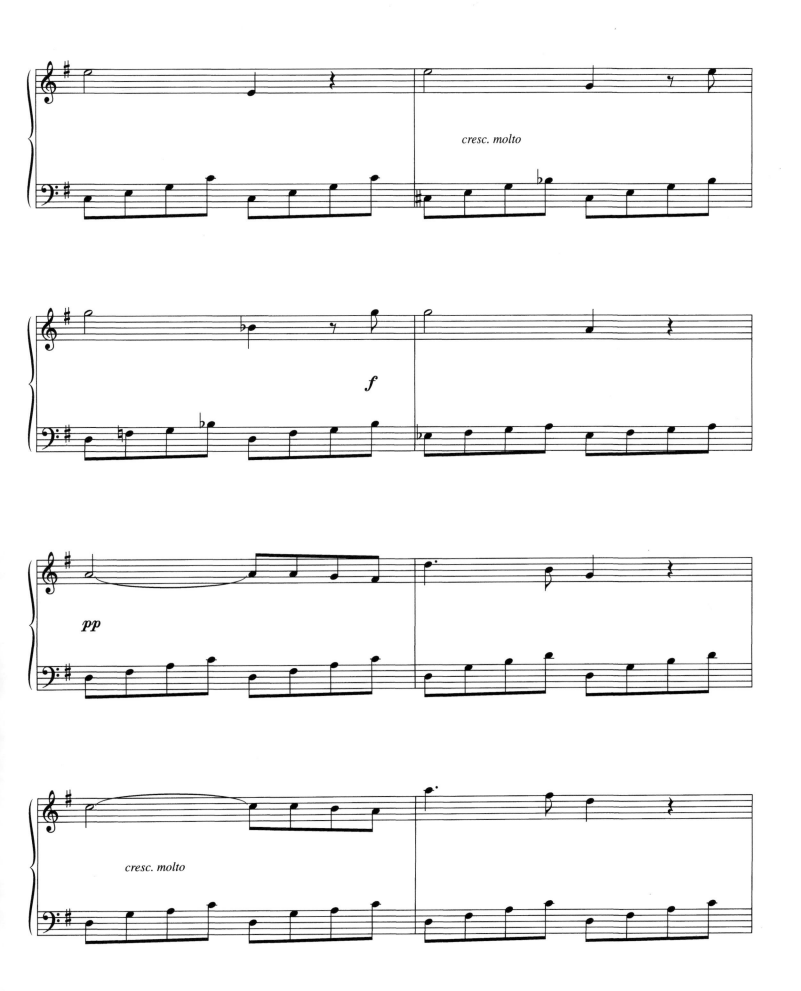

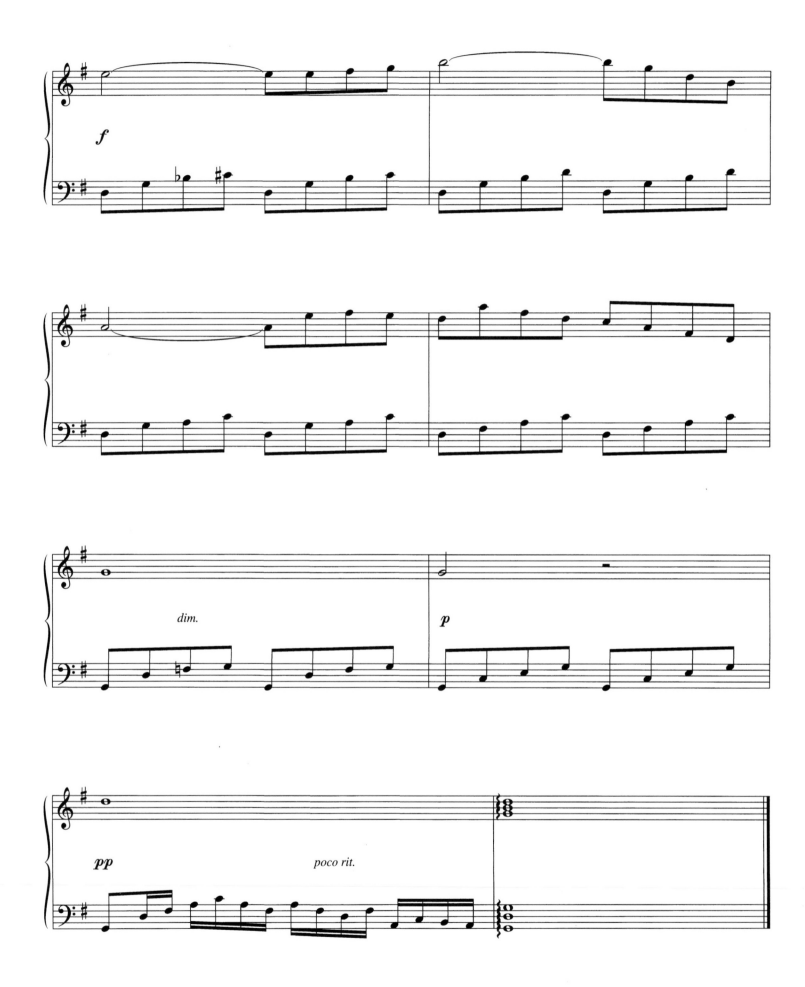

Morning
from PEER GYNT

Edvard Grieg
1843-1907
Op. 23, No. 13
originally for orchestra

Allegretto pastorale

original key: E Major

Solvejg's Song

from PEER GYNT

Edvard Grieg
1843-1907
Op. 23, No. 20
originally for soprano and orchestra

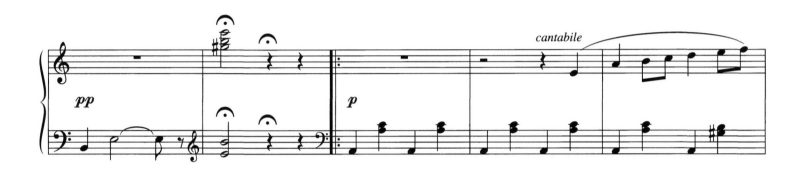

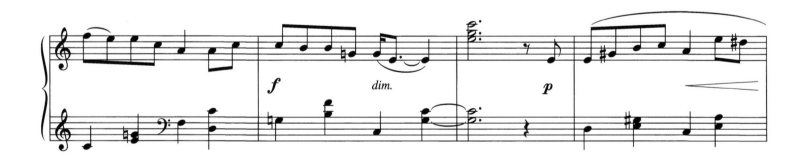

91

Allegro Maestoso
from WATER MUSIC
Excerpt

George Frideric Handel
1685-1759
originally for orchestra

Allegro maestoso

original key: D Major

94

The Trumpet Shall Sound

from MESSIAH

George Frideric Handel
1685-1759
originally for bass, trumpet and orchestra

Pompaso, ma non allegro

original key: D Major

Symphony No. 94

"Surprise"
Second Movement Excerpt

Franz Joseph Haydn
1732-1809
originally for orchestra

Symphony No. 101
"The Clock"
Third Movement Excerpt

Franz Joseph Haydn
1732-1809
originally for orchestra

original key: D Major

Symphony No. 1
"Titan"
Third Movement Opening Theme

Gustav Mahler
1860-1911
originally for orchestra

Solemn and steady, without dragging

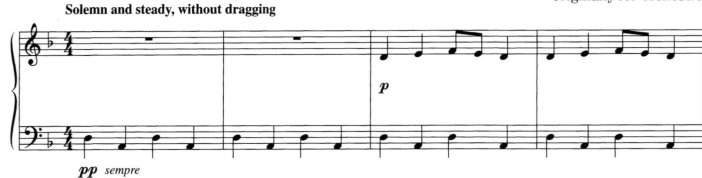

A Midsummer Night's Dream

Overture Themes

Felix Mendelssohn
1809-1847
Op. 61
originally for orchestra

Allegro di molto

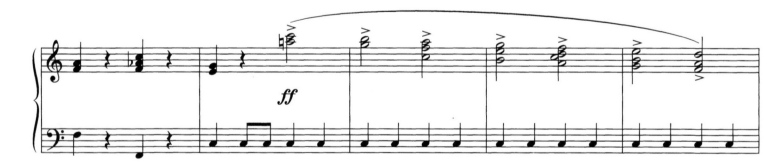

original key: E Major

114

Symphony No. 4
"Italian"
First Movement Excerpt

Felix Mendelssohn
1809-1847
Op. 90
originally for orchestra

original key: A Major

Alleluia
from the solo motet EXSULTATE, JUBILATE
Excerpt

Wolfgang Amadeus Mozart
1756-1791
K 165
originally for soprano and orchestra

Symphony No. 29

First Movement Excerpt

Wolfgang Amadeus Mozart
1756-1791
K 201
originally for orchestra

Allegro moderato

original key: A Major

Symphony No. 35
"Haffner"
First Movement Excerpt

Wolfgang Amadeus Mozart
1756-1791
K 385
originally for orchestra

Allegro con spirito

original key: D Major

Symphony No. 40
First Movement Excerpt

Wolfgang Amadeus Mozart
1756-1791
K 550
originally for orchestra

Allegro molto

original key: G Minor

Eine kleine Nachtmusik
(A Little Night Music)
First Movement Excerpt

Wolfgang Amadeus Mozart
1756-1791
K 525
originally for string ensemble

Barcarolle

from the opera LES CONTES D'HOFFMANN
(The Tales of Hoffmann)

Jacques Offenbach
1819-1880
originally for singers, chorus and orchestra

Moderato

molto cantabile

original key: D Major

141

Rondeau
from the theatre music for ABDELAZER

Henry Purcell
1659-1695
originally for orchestra

* Main theme used by Benjamin Britten in his YOUNG PERSON'S GUIDE TO THE ORCHESTRA

143

D.C. al Fine

Piano Concerto No. 2
First Movement Excerpt

Sergei Rachmaninoff
1873-1943
Op. 18
originally for piano and orchestra

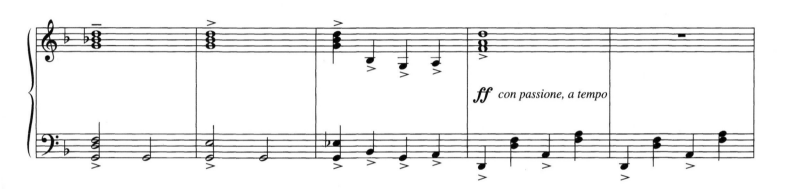

original key: C Minor

William Tell Overture

from the opera GUILLAUME TELL
(William Tell)

Gioachino Rossini
1792-1868
originally for orchestra

original key: E Major

154

Sheherazade
"The Young Prince and Young Princess"
Excerpt

Nikolay Andreyevich Rimsky-Korsakov
1844-1908
Op. 35
originally for orchestra

Andantino quasi Allegretto

Sadko
"Song of India"

Nikolay Andreyevich Rimsky-Korsakov
1844-1908
Op. 5
originally for orchestra

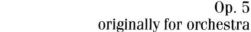

Andantino

p

rit.   *dolce*   *a tempo*

rit.

pp   *sempre legato assai*

Aquarium
from CARNIVAL OF THE ANIMALS

Camille Saint-Saëns
1835-1921
composed 1886
originally for chamber ensemble

Serenade
(Ständchen)

Franz Schubert
1797-1828
D. 957, No. 4
originally for voice and piano

Symphony No. 8

"Unfinished"
First Movement Excerpt

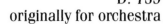

Franz Schubert
1797-1828
D. 759
originally for orchestra

Allegro moderato

original key: B Minor

172

Widmung
(Devotion)

Robert Schumann
1810-1856
Op. 25, No. 1
originally for voice and piano

Tenderly, with spirit (♩ = c. 120)

original key: A-flat Major

Tempo I (♩ = c. 120)

Vienna Life

(Wiener Blut)
Themes

Johann Strauss, Jr.
1825-1899
Op. 354
originally for orchestra

Tempo di Valse

Emperor Waltz
(Kaiser Walzer)
Excerpt

Johann Strauss, Jr.
1825-1899
Op. 437
originally for orchestra

Slow March Tempo

194

196

Piano Concerto No. 1

First Movement Excerpt

Pyotr Il'yich Tchaikovsky
1840-1893
Op. 23
originally for piano and orchestra

Andante maestoso

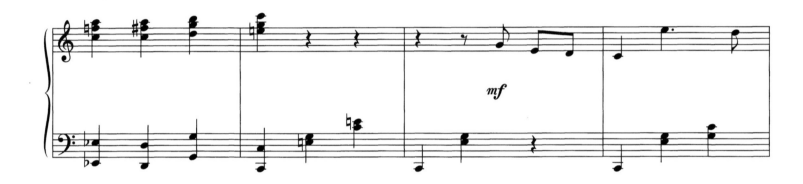

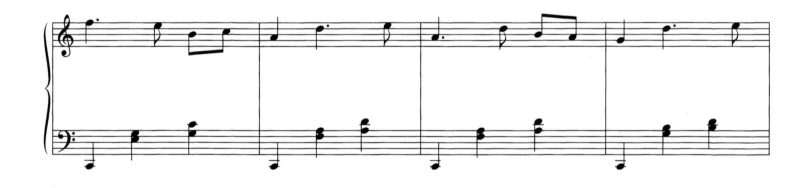

original key: B-flat Major

ROMEO AND JULIET

Fantasy Overture
"Love Theme"

Pyotr Il'yich Tchaikovsky
1840-1893
originally for orchestra

Allegro giusto, con espressione

mf legato e dolce

pp

sim.

original key: D-flat Major

The Sleeping Beauty Waltz

from the ballet THE SLEEPING BEAUTY

Excerpt

Pyotr Il'yich Tchaikovsky
1840-1893
Op. 66
originally for orchestra

Tempo di Valse

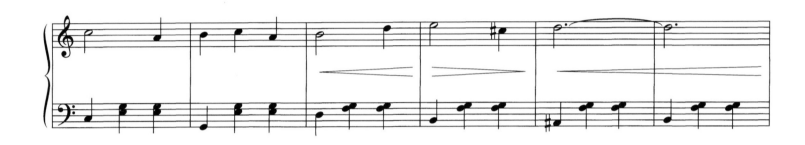

original key: B-flat Major

Waltz of the Flowers

from the ballet THE NUTCRACKER
Excerpt

Pyotr Il'yich Tchaikovsky
1840-1893
Op. 71
originally for orchestra

original key: D Major

Violin Concerto
"L'autunno" (Autumn)
from THE FOUR SEASONS
(a grouping of four violin concertos)
Third Movement

Antonio Vivaldi
1678-1741
RV293, P257, M78, Op. 8, No. 3
originally for violin & string orchestra

226

Violin Concerto
"La primavera" (Spring)

from THE FOUR SEASONS
(a grouping of four violin concertos)
First Movement

Antonio Vivaldi
1678-1741
RV269, P241, M76, Op. 8, No. 1
originally for violin & string orchestra

original key: E Major

229

World's Great Classical Music

This ambitious series is comprised entirely of new editions of some of the world's most beloved classical music.
Each volume includes dozens of selections by the major talents in the history of European art music:
Bach, Beethoven, Berlioz, Brahms, Debussy, Dvořák, Handel, Haydn, Mahler, Mendelssohn, Mozart,
Rachmaninoff, Schubert, Schumann, Tchaikovsky, Verdi, Vivaldi, and dozens of other composers.

Easy to Intermediate Piano

The Baroque Era
00240057 Piano Solo $14.95

Beethoven
00220034 Piano Solo $14.95

The Classical Era
00240061 Piano Solo $14.95

Classical Masterpieces
00290520 Piano Solo $16.99

Easier Piano Classics
00290519 Piano Solo $16.99

Favorite Classical Themes
00220021 Piano Solo $15.95

Great Easier Piano Literature
00310304 Piano Solo $15.99

**Mozart –
Simplified Piano Solos**
00220028 Piano Solo $14.95

Opera's Greatest Melodies
00220023 Piano Solo $14.95

The Romantic Era
00240068 Piano Solo $14.95

Johann Strauss
00220040 Piano Solo $14.95

The Symphony
00220041 Piano Solo $14.95

**Tchaikovsky –
Simplified Piano Solos**
00220027 Piano Solo $14.95

Intermediate to Advanced Piano

Bach
00220037 Piano Solo $14.95

The Baroque Era
00240060 Piano Solo $14.95

Beethoven
00220033 Piano Solo $15.95

The Classical Era
00240063 Piano Solo $14.95

Great Classical Themes
00310300 Piano Solo $14.95

Great Masterworks
00220020 Piano Solo $14.95

Great Piano Literature
00310302 Piano Solo $16.99

Mozart
00220025 Piano Solo $14.99

Opera at the Piano
00310297 Piano Solo $16.95

Piano Classics
00290518 Piano Solo $16.99

Piano Preludes
00240248 Piano Solo $16.95

The Romantic Era
00240096 Piano Solo $14.95

Johann Strauss
00220035 Piano Solo $14.95

The Symphony
00220032 Piano Solo $14.95

Tchaikovsky
00220026 Piano Solo $14.95

Instrumental

The Baroque and Classical Flute
00841550 Flute and Piano....................$16.95

Masterworks for Guitar
00699503 Classical Guitar $16.95

The Romantic Flute
00240210 Flute and Piano....................$14.99

Vocal

Gilbert & Sullivan
00740142 Piano/Vocal $19.99

Prices, content, and availability
subject to change without notice.